VINCENT FERRINI

SELECTED POEMS

Edited, with an introduction, by
GEORGE F. BUTTERICK

Storrs, Conn.
The University of Connecticut Library

1976

811
F 392s

Copyright © 1941, 1943, 1944, 1946, 1949, 1950, 1953, 1954, 1955, 1957, 1963, 1967, 1975, 1976 by Vincent Ferrini. All rights reserved.

Printed in the United States of America.

Library of Congress Catalog Card Number 76-43360
ISBN 0-917590-00-7

Most of the poems in this volume have been selected from the following books by Vincent Ferrini: *No Smoke* (Falmouth Publishing House), *Injunction* (Sand Piper Publishers), *Blood of the Tenement* (Sand Piper Publishers), *The Plow in the Ruins* (Decker Press), *Tidal Wave* (Great Concord Publishers), *Sea Sprung* (Cape Ann Press), *The Infinite People* (Great Concord Publishers), *The House of Time* (Fortune Press), *In the Arriving* (Heron Press), *Mindscapes* (Peter Pauper Press), *The Square Root of In* (Heuretic Press), *Mirandum* (Heuretic Press), *I Have the World* (Fortune Press), *The Hiding One* (Me and Thee Press) and *Ten Pound Light* (The Church Press). Others have previously appeared in the following publications, to which grateful acknowledgement is also made: *Athanor*, *Gloucester Daily Times*, *North Shore*. "Oud Song," "Asteroids," "An Auspice," "Ballad of the Possessed," "After Reading Yeats," "A Weak Lamp," "Rock Village," "Spades," and "Paean of Joy" are published here for the first time.

Publication of this volume has been made possible by the support of the friends of Vincent Ferrini.

PHOTO by ARNIE JARMAK

80-10090

Library of Davidson College

VOID

For my believers

CONTENTS

INTRODUCTION

NO SMOKE (1941)
    The City
    Jeffery Tallcott
    Razor Blades
    Floyd Hecket
    George Dangerfield
    Myer Levy
    Henry Kiely
    Peter Joyce
    Matthew Byrne
    Harmon Cleveland
    Tanney Bronson
    Nora Omen
    George Alkaluvious
    The Factories

INJUNCTION (1943)
    Fluoroscope of Evening
    Workshops in Labor
    The Gates Admit Snapshots
    In the Cage of Phobia
    Skeleton in the Mind
    The Dead Hours Are Tall Lampposts
    The City with Empty Closets
    Letter to my Brother
    Smoke Dreams with Harlequin
    Forge Plant
    The Locusts
    Talking Tenements

BLOOD OF THE TENEMENT (1944)
    First Furrowing
    Grief Sits on the Windowsill
    For Our Daily Bread
    The Reign of Beasts
    Locked in Bed with Bronchitis and the Doctor Has Left with the Key
    Quarrel
    Nerves Hanging Over Telephone Wires
    Live Cemeteries
    Wine of the Heart

THE PLOW IN THE RUINS (1946)
    Photograph of Starved Child Dumped in a Burial Cart
    In the Wake of the Vultures
    The Ballad of the Black Idea

TIDAL WAVE: POEMS OF THE GREAT STRIKES (1946)
    Twilight and Sunrise
    To the Legislators

SEA SPRUNG (1949)
    Fishcutters

THE INFINITE PEOPLE (1950)
    Folksong
    Discovery
    The History of a Sheet on a Clothesline

THE HOUSE OF TIME (1953)
>   Transmigration
>   A Little Autobiography
>   Where I once was . . .
>   Lament
>   The Tiny Room

IN THE ARRIVING (1954)
>   Section 5

MINDSCAPES (1955)
>   Selections

THE SQUARE ROOT OF IN (1957)
>   Selections

MIRANDUM (1963)
>   Suddenly space . . .
>   A mad one . . .
>   Joy! . . .
>   The passing . . .
>   It is the lightning . . .
>   At wake . . .

I HAVE THE WORLD (1967)
>   The Other Side
>   The Garden of the Apocalypse
>   The Gold

UNCOLLECTED AND UNPUBLISHED POEMS (1968-1975)
  Oud Song
  Asteroids
  An Auspice
  Ballad of the Possessed
  After Reading Yeats
  The Tides
  Spades
  A Weak Lamp
  Rock Village
  The *theia mania* of Charles Olson
  Paean of Joy for the Birth of a Church
  The Night the Harbor Fill Sat on the Community
    Fish Pier Table

THE HIDING ONE (1973)
  Lenin Speaks
  In the Wake of Night I Beheld the Generations
  The Two Harbors of Gloucester
  First Freak Village
  Tongue II

TEN POUND LIGHT (1975)
  Eleven

INTRODUCTION

By the time Charles Olson looked Vincent Ferrini up in 1949 to compliment him on the poems he had published in the magazine *Imagi* (including the one on p. 56 of this selection), Ferrini had already published five books of poems (to Olson's one). Ferrini might be remembered in American literary history for Olson's attack on him in *The Maximus Poems* as the editor of *Four Winds*, or even for his longlasting friendship with Charles Olson. And it is true that he was the catalyst that brought together Olson and Robert Creeley to begin that most important of recent literary friendships; who "invoked" the Maximus poems themselves, begun as a series of letters to him, by being the presence in Gloucester whom Olson could confidently address; the man whom Olson would come to call his only "brother" despite the crushing attack earlier; and who in later years would succeed Olson as the conscience of Gloucester and public voice for the preservation of her values. But it must also be recognized that Vincent Ferrini is very much a poet in his own right, one who offers distinct pleasure to a variety of readers, and who has lived, to the best of his ability, what might be called the life of a poet, outside of schools and spheres of influence, for more than forty years.

Ferrini's poems, although they did not create an age of poetry the way Olson's did, or Pound's had, certainly reflect with accuracy and courage the ages the poet has passed through. They can be read as a history of our time: the anxieties and grinding poverty of industrial America, immigrant America, Depression America, up through the age which followed the economic boom after World War II with its concomitant luxury of expanded consciousness. His poems do not extend the limits of language or create an alternative world, but they do humanize the present one. In precisely this way, the course of his career is of interest and the poet's own persistence in following his vocation rewarded. Ferrini began as an authentic proletarian writer, a worker, largely self-educated, writing about the people for the people. Mike Gold, author of that classic of the Depression, *Jews Without Money*, said of Ferrini's early poems that they were as "genuine as a soldier's wound or a row of stamping machines," and Walter Lowenfels rightly identified him as "the last surviving Proletarian Poet." Then, as the bonds which gripped him relaxed somewhat over the years, his writing extended into poems of relationships governed not by economic necessities but cosmic fates, astral reckonings and passions, mystical adventurings. In many of the later poems, symbols float, images abound but they are no longer bound to their subject. Blakean phrases and ethereal suggestions appear as they have not before: "celestial earthlings," "a mating of contraries," "the Crucible of the Unseen," "the Subtleties of the Spirit," have replaced the paycheck, the smokestacks, the Welfare, the shoe lasts and forges. The poet's belief that "the working of the imagination is Divinity in the process of realizing itself" gained strength, seemed to find confirmation. There is an amplification of spirit in poems such as "The Garden of the Apocalypse" and "Tongue II," made possible by the deepest human tenderness of earlier poems like "Discovery" and "The Tiny Room," from a poet who has never denied his roots.

    The poet was born Venanzio, after the patron saint of his father's town, in 1913, in the industrial city of Lynn, Massachusetts, northeast of Boston. He was the child of immigrants, part of that great wave reaching these shores in 1909. His father was a Christian anarchist from Raiano in central Italy, his mother from Bella further to the south. Lynn at that time was the largest manufacturer of shoes in the world, and his father was a shoeworker, like Nicola Sacco. The boy grew up in Sacco and Vanzetti's Massachusetts, among dumps and tidal creeks, the salt of the tenements. Laconia Court in Lynn was literally a dead-end street up against the Boston and Maine Railroad tracks surrounded by brickyards. "The terrible winters," the poet remembers, "snows six feet high. My mother heating the andiron, wrapping a towel around it and placing it under my feet, going to the Welfare office for foodstamps. I am dragging over ice and snow the 100 pound bags of coal from Lamper's Wharf. I am guarding my baby sister in her highchair by the stove when it explodes, kills her, gashes my arm and forehead, my brother Dante under the stove, escaping, and I am crying my heart out, 'What are we going to do about Yolanda, what are we to be without her,' the doctor stitching my arm up, and the corner of my eye." He had seen that the dumps could contain the naked dead body of an infant; there were brushes with the law over some silver bullion in a warehouse; one summer he was harnessed to a stitching machine at a shoe factory. Was there to be an alternative? During high school he discovered Shelley (as later Gregory Corso would), but his father told him insistently: "You can't be a poet, you are born in the wrong class. You are the son of a shoemaker, you will work for a living like I do!" These are the forces—a burning romanticism and the inescapable reality of daily work—that will be with him throughout all his poetry (and his life, for that matter), never fully reconciled.

    He graduated from high school, barely (he had shown his poems to the head of the English department and her verdict was flat: "You will never be a poet"), but his real education, his real degree, was from the Lynn Public Library. It was to be a period of turmoil, worthy of a Shelleyan poet. His hair was at his shoulders; his father, disturbed he is bringing attention to himself, scolds, "When are you going to get a haircut." He is intense, "fanatic" in his own words. Only books are real. He wears a long black coat down to his ankles and a black fedora hat, carrying a black bag which he fills up with library books that he cannot bear to part with. He accumulates a library of his own from the public library, his bedroom lined to the ceiling with the books. He emerges from his solitary cell only to eat, and, without a word, goes back. There he lives with Socrates, Sophocles, Shakespeare. Finally, after two years, stricken with guilt and remorse, he returns the books intermittently. He packs the books in his black bag and nervously tucks them back into the military rows, keeping an eye cocked, until the last link of the chain of guilt falls from him.

At the library and on the street corners his politics continued to take shape. Saturday night discussions at the house of Truman Nelson (the "Tanney Bronson" of *No Smoke*), who would later publish books on John Brown and William Lloyd Garrison, clarified issues and provided exposure to a wider range of social ideas. As the Depression wore on, he managed to secure a job with the WPA working on log books at the Peabody Museum in Salem, discovering what American vessels touched islands in the Pacific first. After that project came to an end, he was accepted in a teacher's project, where each instructor was responsible for assembling his own classes. During this time he began publishing his poems in literary magazines such as *New Anvil* and *Smoke* (including one poem in the latter under the nom de plume Vincent Ferrous). Until Olson's attack on *Four Winds*, the little magazines were to be his hope and encouragement.

Ferrini's first book, *No Smoke*, published in 1941 shortly before the United States entered World War II, was a series of portraits of seventy-seven citizens of Lynn from all walks of life, with the factories themselves appearing at the end as a character, not as hated oppressor but as the opportunity for a new order. It is a *Spoon River Anthology*, only of the industrial northeast. It could be an Erie or Scranton, New London or Fall River. The smoke of its title would have been a symbol, but no esoteric one, to the people of Lynn: the smudge hung in the sky was the evidence of factories alive—of work, wages, families fed, housed, and clothed; while the dreaded absence of it meant the opposite—shut-downs, lay-offs, lock-outs, strikes, plants moving South to cheaper labor, and the privations almost immediately felt, or read in the eyes. The author had originally written the poems using the actual names of persons, but the publisher, fearing libel, refused to issue the book that way. Even so, the poems were too uncomfortably real for some of the citizens, despite the "disclaimer" that "Any similarity in this book to the names of persons living or dead is coincidental," and the copy in the local public library, which had made it possible in the first place, was kept locked in the reference room where it was available only by special request.

His next books, written throughout the 1940's while he was working full time at the General Electric factory — where his tasks included rolling sheets of aircraft linen into vats for making tape and salvaging copper wire from scrap — continue to reflect an intense social consciousness. *Injunction*, which Mike Gold praised at length in the *Daily Worker*, offers a series of working class vignettes with the War as backdrop; *Blood of the Tenements* are fierce poems of urban love; *The Plow in the Ruins* reflects the ruins of war; and *Tidal Wave* is a series written with sleeves rolled up for the picket line.

At this time, a painter living up the coast in Gloucester named Louis Evan (shortened from Evangelista) paid Ferrini a fan visit in Lynn, after reading Gold's praise in the *Worker*. Ferrini returned the visit and was so captivated by Gloucester, the city of fishermen, that, despite the precariousness of finding housing for three small children, in January 1948 he and his wife made the move to 3 Liberty Street, although he continued to work at GE, commuting by train and with a group by car. During this time, too, he quit what he referred to as "the Church of Politics." It was too doctrinaire for a poet: "The organizers come in from Boston and New York, and explain the line. There is discussion, but the decisions are preordained like a papal encyclical. The roots of the Party are in Russia, and they have an alien smell." When Evan decided to move to New York and sell his small house that had once been a barroom, Ferrini's brother Dante bought it. In the back the painter had run a small frame shop, and before he left he convinced the poet to learn the trade and become a picture-framer. That August, nine months short of ten years at GE and eligibility for a pension (which would come to haunt him in later years), Ferrini quit the factory and became a frame-maker. He was his own boss at last, although never free from the pressure of having to support himself by his hands, week after week, year upon year. For the rest of his life, Ferrini has remained a frame-maker, with all the puns possible from that—the years in service to others' art, the delimiter of art, the final arbiter, provider of perspective, enhancer—his own needs as a creative intelligence in constant tension with the need to earn a living. The final poem of this selection, more than twenty-five years later, still has it as a theme.

With the factories of Lynn behind him, with a wider sky, on an earth he could love, and the new horizon of the sea, the poems, too, extended out. He wrote plays, two of which were selected for the *Best Short Plays* of 1952–1953 and 1953–1954. His poems appeared in many of the wondrously named little magazines of the day—*Golden Goose, Glass Hill, Suck-Egg Mule, Naked Ear, Combustion, Goad, View, Mutiny, Angry Penguins, Artisan, Gryphon, Beloit Poetry Journal, Origin, Vou, Contact.* He and others in Gloucester undertook a magazine of their own, *Four Winds,* which lasted for three issues. It disappointed and angered Charles Olson, who berated Ferrini in "Letter 5" of *The Maximus Poems* for what he saw as a carelessness betraying the dignity of Gloucester. Ferrini intended his *In the Arriving* to be his "answer" to Olson. It offered, as the section included here exemplifies, only love, the other cheek.

Vincent Ferrini has continued to write throughout these years, seeking to frame the universe, always acknowledging the tensions within it, loving the self-replenishing paradox, whether in the haiku-inspired koans from *Mindscapes* and *The Square Root of In*, or the restlessly moving later poems, sweeping the Cape Ann landscape like the beacon of the lighthouse on Ten Pound Island in Gloucester Harbor which provides the title for his most recent collection. It is all one, the life and art, if it can be discovered. This is what he meant by the title of his book *The Hiding One*. It is for the reader to bring out, to discover the poem as being all in a day's work, the struggle by the master frame-maker to shape the wood of words as readily as he could the other wood with his hands.

    These poems have been selected from fifteen of Vincent Ferrini's over twenty books, many of which were self-published and consequently might otherwise be lost, or at least not widely available. Included is a small section of poems written in the period 1968–1975 which either were never published or appeared only in periodicals. The selection covers the full span of the poet's career, from 1941 through 1975, displaying the development of a singular American poet as he responds to changes in the world surrounding him.

GEORGE F. BUTTERICK

THE CITY

15 years ago this city was the shoe hub of the world.
160 factories hummed a song of joy.
Jobs were so plentiful you tripped over them.
And our families had happiness.
Today the city is a graveyard of factories—
Monumental tombstones accusing with broken eyes.
A jungle of death pregnant with another life.
And we shoeworkers
Idly mushroom the union halls arguing.
Skeptical of the future, we talk of the past:
Of the crowded union meetings,
The honest speeches inspiring guts to sacrifice,
The monster demonstrations and the unbreakable strikes.
6 months ago the last giant factory
Said 'Accept a 20% cut.'
The Union answered 'NO!'
The Boss grabbed his shop and settled out of the state
Leaving 1700 families stranded.
The Union caved in.
At dawn busses and cars carry shoeworkers
    to far-away open shop towns.
And we thousands remaining
Huddled in tenements
Starve in the shadows of dead factories.

JEFFERY TALLCOTT

Each morning my wife guides me
Through a black city to Union Street.
I tune my old violin and my wife
Returns home with the case.
My tapping stick is my eyes.
I play and sing to the people buzzing
      and bumping into me.
I love my clay pipe.
Every hour I shake my tin can to hear
If we'll have enough to eat.
It rains and I sing by a doorway.
The look in my eyes begging is an unknown story.
Mid-afternoon and the tinkle of one nickel.
Dupont gave me
The only hundred dollars I ever had
When I lost my eyes mixing paints for him.
My face pleading these many years
      is a sculptured torture.
The hot sun is like my wife's love.
My voice tires and I play a jig.
The dust of the street fills the wrinkles in my cheeks.
Why don't those other beggars die?
They'll only queer my territory.
Day after day I strain to hear a tinkle.
All they see is blotches of blood on the face I shaved at
And holes in my pants.
Saturday music of dimes, pennies and nickels
Dropping in my tin can
Is the only happiness I know.
The snow and ice and whipping wind
Freeze my feet, my fingers, and my voice
And I am a corpse with a can on my chest.
When the streets quiet and death
Is punctured by the click of shoes
And ripped by the swish of automobiles
My wife comes to take me home.

RAZOR BLADES

The wind cuts through his ragbag coat.
Toes frozen in sorry shoes.
He peddles razor blades and French safes
On the streets.
Once had a job in the G.E.
And dressed like success.
Crippled eyes wander for a sale:
With face of a YMCA secretary.
People shun him—
Say he hasn't got all his marbles.
He loiters at tavern doors
To empty eager sales.
Moans he's got a pain in the leg.
Nightly haunts cafes table to table
Seeking couples for sales.
Once sent up for softening of the brain.
Like a fugitive
He roams the streets at midnight
Bound nowhere,
Carrying on a conversation with himself.
In cafes he shatters the air
With his dying till they buy him a drink.
Drowning himself in the harbor
They fished him back to life.

FLOYD HECKET

In mackinaw born with a cigar in his mouth.
The substantial pillar of the city.
Voice like a burlesque comedian.
He retires on his secret knowledge
Of Who's Who and What's What
With a tired indifference
Which is a halo in a crowd of looks.
Face is a fried egg swimming in oil.
You've got to be in his intimate circle
To warrant a glance from his municipal eye.
If you want to sail into the uncertain
      weather of politics
See a friend of his to get you the dope
Or an introduction.
Is a smoke stack with 15 daily cigars.
His statements are gems
To be recorded in a new history of the city.
Known from one end to another
As the political sage of Central Square.
What he doesn't know isn't worth knowing.
His office hours at Huntts' restaurant
8 p.m. to 1 a.m.

GEORGE DANGERFIELD

All flashed up:
Wide brimmed green felt hat
With newspaper brains under it,
Starched collar and green necktie,
Peg bottom trousers,
Black Cuban shoes,
And green form–fitting jacket
With trick pockets.
Handsome as a movie star.
Promenades up and down
Night after night on Central Square
Like a loud sonata.
Flashes a lewd look
Or a bored one.
His ambition is fulfilled:
Has more clothes than Beau Brummell had.
Never works.
Knows what horse to bet on,
How to talk to women.
Girls eye him with desire
And date him.
Adopted the name of a plutocrat,
Imitates his accent
And is on the make
For girls with money.
Other fellows sneer jealously,
Call him queer
Or copy him.

MYER LEVY

Read so many books
He lost himself.
Boys marvel at his knowledge
Till they get stuck in a swamp.
Today he sells a device for filling teeth
Without going to a dentist,
Tomorrow a plan to vision the old City Hall
      as a new one.
His head is a lumber yard.
Argues to influence other people—
Burping new angles to a problem you're sick of.
So busy thinking of what he's going to say
He doesn't hear you.
Can't resist temptation to paw a
      girl on first acquaintance.
If lucky to hook a job
He sells himself out of it.
From island to island at the all night cafeteria,
Burning ears.
Mouthing a 5 cent cigar he feels like an executive.
Wobbles like he's looking for himself.
He nabs you in the street and pumps
      you full of a new gadget
He fell over in a new magazine.
Expects to become a millionaire some day.
At public dances rubs his genitals against girls' legs to
      wet his pants.
His father once worried, is resigned.
They don't talk to each other.

Their heads have potato bumps from trying to sell
 each other opposite ideas.
Lives on his father's old age pension.
Worms his nose in a private toilet of sex books.
Over and over he wonders
Why he can't get a girl
And he flogs himself.
Is now selling
Faith in One's Self,
The religion he discovered
The people need.

HENRY KIELY

Struts like a tin soldier
With his head in a cock's tilt.
Believes he's the link
Between politicians and the people.
Gets the *Congressional Record* by special delivery.
Want to know what strings to pull
You ought to see him.
His command of English is the sorrow of a cat.
Everybody calls him 'Senator'
And he loves to hear it.
Don't get tough with him—
Your name won't be worth birds' droppings.
Life is a chess game and he's the trick hand:
Hasn't missed a move yet.
Floats in expectancy of a government job
That's always due any day.
In suspended dread someone will find out
He's a broken down would-be ward heeler.

PETER JOYCE

Never wears a hat.
Fishscaled with money,
He talks to Christ
Because he's scared of death.
Taxis drive him to Mass at 6 o'clock each morning.
Holy crucifixes,
Beads and medals
Protect his chest.
Takes mumbo jumbo notes at football games
He doesn't understand.
And walks the streets praying for the next life.

MATTHEW BYRNE

The wisdom of great men
Is grooved on his cerebellum.
In the streets he quotes
Shakespeare and the Bible
To answer the times.
Thirsty eyes drink people's souls
And buried secrets.
His Irish talk is a forest brook.
Doesn't know where the money
Is coming from to keep him alive
Next week.
Creeps with eagle haunches
20 miles to hear an orator
And dreams of the priest
He might have been.

HARMON CLEVELAND

So healthy you want to eat him
But the taste throws up on you.
Yesses everybody.
His office smells of hypocrisy
And is always open to the public.
'Yes, yes, we'll do what we can
But the power's with the School Committee.'
Any protest upsets him, squirming and
      blubbering excuses.
Looks forward to graduation to pass blessed diplomas
Serious as a seal.
Addressing an assembly
You feel the dignity of Babbitt.
He tests every sentence in an acid bath of hems
      and haws.
With hunted look he pokes his head
In the office of his lieutenant for permission.
Summers he studies Europe.
Thinks it is one jump from school to the Rotary Club.
His porky income is legislated to the winds.
Nods 'how-do-you-do—can't stop to talk just now.'
Breathes a mortal terror the social order will collapse
And his life-savings vanish.

TANNEY BRONSON

Everything his protean brain touches he
    breathes to life.
Rooted in the revolution of 1776.
Palms calloused by pick and shovel
On the pulse of the people
Are fists full of liberty.
Poetry spills from his lips
And his consciousness is a sleepless eye.
When he imitates people your stomach
    knots with laughter.
His criticisms cut the legs under you.
Hammers the time as it happens into songs
    for workers' ears.
Old clothes need him.
His head is a faun's.
Friend to square pegs in round holes.
Honest as the sting of truth
And suffers for it.
In his house there is free speech.
Wherever he is the air blossoms,
Exciting you with a drama of stories,
Unending jokes and anecdotes.
His rooms are splashed with paintings.
You are reborn when you hear him freeing music
And around his fireplace you chew a bit
    of greatness.
With him you become an explorer,
The dormant universe electrified within you.
His blood throbs with the untaught American past,
Bringing it back to the people.

NORA OMEN

A 10 cent wedding ring tied the nuptial knot.
Their bed is the Welfare
And their rooms rest on quicksand.
Her hatchet nose defies all enemies
And eyes spit fire,
Blunt as a sledge blow on fingers.
Organizes mothers on her street to strike for low rent,
And committees to cut the price of milk and bread;
They never knew how before and it works,
And they love her for it.
Visits them bringing gifts of leaflets
      and pamphlets with answers.
She sails into offices of the Powers That Be
And rocks the roof of their smugness.
Get smart with her and your head's in pincers.
Quickest time to get results is a straight line of attack.
Persistent as a flood,
Her words and manners punch you in the nose.
Offers no excuse
And changes her tactics.
Loses herself and evolves
New ways of living.
Loving this life fiercely for what it must become.

GEORGE ALKALUVIOUS

20 years I worked this machine.
Millions of shoes took the shape of my feeder;
My foot wore the peddle to a shiny steel.
Resting at noon with dry sandwiches and card games.
The times I slaved with the electric bulb
Piercing and blinding my eyes—
The operations repeating in my sleep.
These tools know only my hands
And the machine intimate as my wife's body.
And now, 'Sorry we can't use you
Any longer. Too old. Too slow.'
Can they take the callouses out of my hands;
Make me see with these opera glasses;
Iron the hill on my back
And the twist in my side
And wipe the ache of it off
And pay me back what I really earned?
They can't rob the best years of my life
And then throw me out in the gutter
Like a dirty rag.
This machine and this job belongs
To me more than it does to the Boss.

THE FACTORIES

Sunsets splash blood in our broken eyes
And the moon splinters.
Dead, we are huge and ugly
With derelict canyons between.
Our floors empty as Sunday,
Abandoned by the Bosses
And a few abusing us.
Our skeleton teeth locked on the sky.
Workers,
It is not our fault you starve
Idle without purpose.
Workers, resurrect us—
Put life back into our hollow bodies!
Let us breathe again
And the word 'fired' be a nightmare that
     died with the past
And for the first time own your jobs!
The Union to operate us for the good of the people
And the profits divided among you
To build a city of love!
Fill us with the bubble of bustle:
Your tools clicking a chorus of work
Stitching leather into shoes for the feet of the people,
Laughter splitting the air!
Human voices warm with intimate happiness
Exciting our veins and arteries and cold floors!
We'll feel we are wanted!
We'll drink your singing at the machines,
Wait for your coming daily!
And glow with the jagged electricity of seasonal picnics!
We won't hurt you with accidents!
No more speed-up torturing the nerves
     and the bottled anger!

And no Bosses cracking the whip of low prices!
Patch us up and air-condition our lungs!
Shoes you make will be your own
And you'll love them like works of beauty!
And the reality of the 5 hour day!
Invented machines ending drudgery
And pouring leisure into your laps!
And the wages will buy you your own homes!
Your example will be a fuse leading to
      coffin cities and ghost towns,
Igniting the people to possession—to free America!
Think! Believe it!
You've got nothing to lose but your poverty
And the creative life that should be yours will begin!
Time rots us and buries you.
O workers, we are yours for the taking.
For what are you waiting?

FLUOROSCOPE OF EVENING

Telephone wires are secret
The streets dry rivers

A few old men support the corners
And taverns have the look of deserted women

The newsboy's voice is a lunatic
      screeching against the stars

The ice-cream parlor has one light on
The lampposts have bandages on their eyes

No automobile horn calls for a girl
Poolroom tables are half awake

Those not out are sleeping for the
      next day's work

Some windows tell you how it is
You never noticed so many strangers before

They have all gone but the memory
The city is a ghost house with many corridors.

WORKSHOPS IN LABOR

Who what who what who what mmmmm what
    sings the boring mill
Sput sput sput drrrrr the pneumatic drill
Shattering nerves and losing clothes
Swish wish swish ssss quick brush off of the air hose
The hammers on steel ring Independence bells
Mee ow mee ow mee ow
Ah Oooooo Ah ooooo and the yells
Of the workers' eyes caressing the girls
zzzzzzz of the lathe shedding curls
Thud thud thud of stock
Sudden machine burst and the shock
Telephones rattle persistent as babies bawling
Steam pipes are express trains mauling
Metal sheets clang
Presses click and bang bang
Sewers smoking
Elevators croaking
Fingers in motors drone
And belts moan
Boilers quaking ears
Caskets of casings like biers
Fog horn mooing for help
And sprinkler showering the hollow of rubber kelp
Gears are wailing women at a funeral
Stab of the lunch whistles stall the tempo
Immediately the grind wheels race on a dry track
And machine guns crack
At every minute
The hum is a front at the rear and we're in it
Signals exploding blood cells

Electric saws in aluminum splitting atoms of the air
Hornet buzz of coils and care
Heels and mallets pound foundry soot soft as moonlight
Coal smudges on bodies spoon bright
Blue pain of the acetylene torch tearing the flesh.
The hands whiz like flies in a mesh
Castings thrown in basins like breaking bottles
The blast of furnace throttles
Ovens with hot angry tongues of the captured sun
Zoom at goggles and sweat and everyone
A perpetual feud or a grudge
Like the rumpus after the sentence of a judge
Sandpapers scratch the brain
Jokes grow like grain bring thunder and hidden rain
Workers are metronomes almost without breath
And if machines stop the silence is death

THE GATES ADMIT SNAPSHOTS

Waves of rain pregnant clouds
Over wet morning grass
Razors of the wind cut through flesh lodge in the bone
Trees reach for the sky naked and alone
Like the bowels of graves exposed.
The plants busy as beehives.
From dark towns and cities streams of cars
     speed headlong
For a stall.
Now come the liquid mass of sleep walkers.
Multitudinous as ants crawling over each other
Like the beginning of a river
Eating up the road.
Buttons on collars are identity.
The boy pulls his loaded newspaper cart
     as if it were a bad dream.
Headlines drop depth bombs upon us.
The guard at the gate is a sunflower
Or a tower of ice.

IN THE CAGE OF PHOBIA

23 and dreading the board's decision

"I love life
I wanta live"

Scouts in lunch box
Finds mince meat and slams it into the garbage pail
He could almost stone her
And munches the lettuce and bread
Creeps behind your ears with "ha ha ha
There'll always be an England"

Filing truss rings like a chipmunk
His head churning hate into a cheese
A Jew instinctively smells and cowers
Raises a voltage of anger and chained fists
Or plays the lackey to him

When the boys confide to each other
His high strung laughter snaps and sparks

"You're a Red
You eat Dorothy Thompson before working"

"The army'll knock it out of him!"

"I got flat feet" sliding a sheet under his
    arch "ha ha ha"

The morning papers pour oil upon the
    embers of his neurosis

The gas of anti-semitism
Exceeds saturation

SKELETON IN THE MIND

Raises grew to our names out of deadlock
Congress knits laws against us and chains the air
And our bonds make tanks bombs and bayonets
Prices eat our pocketbooks and we swear.

It was the Union which glued the people together
The pincers of the working class,
That got us vacations with pay, wages and hours
But it was War that put to work the mass.

These envelopes have the worms of Depression in them
Food is rationed, shadows of no work and fear
Stick to our thoughts and we scrimp dollars
Against the time that will too soon be here.

THE DEAD HOURS ARE TALL LAMPPOSTS

The moonlight is an enamel table top
The house is an egg at the edge of it
And the hum of automobile tires on the pavement
The approaching bombers.

THE CITY WITH EMPTY CLOSETS

The sidewalks are the ribs of a skeleton
A new people are everywhere
The shadow of the bridge lengthens
And a crow stabs at the autumn twilight
The Security Trust is a closed temple
Movies gulp women
A chill wind and the streets become alien
The tide is full with the unknown future
Dried blood of leaves are the nails
      of dogs running on concrete.
The draft has picked the city clean
      as a chicken bone.

LETTER TO MY BROTHER

The umbilical cord connects us both to Ma and America
The front your bayonet sticks into is secret
And what you suffer are pins in my imagination
As my fingers sharpen the animus of superchargers.
Like fanatics the others sweat the machines
Silent with the same thoughts
Or probably scarred.
Weeks melt into months
And the months are moving in the second year
And for you too it is a long time
Must we wait till their gunbutts break down our doors
Lindo there are enemies in our midst
Their paws on the buttons of power
With monkeywrenches in production and unity
Plotting against you and the common people
O let them beware the whirlwinds of our anger
Lindo let hate be your science
And spit at the gargoyles of danger
Those who reach us with their eggs
Like gnarled trees
We'll thrust our hands into the sky
And bash their pregnant bodies together
For the weapons we send you
And your bayonet
Will anneal the People's Revolutions
And you come back to a country where Ma and our
      kids won't ever go to the Welfare again.

SMOKE DREAMS WITH HARLEQUIN

When the whistle blows
It disembowels the clock
You're on your own
Like a frog on a rock
So the lunch hour flows

Together and alone
Team up for bocci
Hey Frankie ought she
Those at craps
See their maps
Grow
Or shrink in woe
Goosey is lucky at darts
But fly when he farts
Nose in newspapers
Make queer wallpapers
Girls dance and knit
Or give the same to a fresh guy's wit
Get the inside news
At horseshoes
He'd rather play poker
Than stroke her
The tired cook in the sun
Forgetting work to be done.

Till swift as knowledge of a loss
The gizzards of the clock
Spring together again
De-atomizing women and men
For long or short walk:
The sticky ones feel the Boss.

FORGE PLANT

Insects with antlers
And iron shoes
Their eyes peer out of asbestos boxes
Pushing 2 ton stock
Red as sunrise
Out of yellow volcanoes of furnaces
To be cut and shaped by 9 ton electric hammers
Black workers
White workers
Looking alike with dirt and oil
And the women in amber rooms polishing cutting filing
And the fussy jobs of grinders at the edge of the storm
Look how they feed the hot metal into mighty intestines
Pounding them into moulds
In a shower of stars
Kneading thunder
And lightning and the strength and secrets of the
      universe!
Like gods at the bins of forges
Wetting the birdfeet with swab
By the trigger thud thud thud thud
O workers nothing is impossible for you
Pounders of the tongues of ships
The guts of holocaust!
Unconscious O workers of your genius
And now wielding your power and grasp like giants!
Energies paid by War
Why have you never worked like this in Peace time?

THE LOCUSTS

Comb the hair of the skies with our searchlights of fingers
And crush them like lice with our thumbnails!

TALKING TENEMENTS

37,000 blades of wheat
Bound by a wire of union
Keep bread for 130,000 mouths

One man is a leaf in the gutter kicked by winter

One man is an atom of sand
37,000 are a brick

And thousands of bricks
Between the Atlantic and Pacific discover
A country of no rich
And no poor

No one listens to you or me
But They become ears when WE talk

The will of the majority is a road
And the law backs us up

We've travelled right to the jaws of the abyss
The enemy undermines the air we live on

After our kin kill the fascists
And our sons brothers and husbands die

With who return
We must bridge the abyss
Those in Power will say
No the works belong to them

But we are used to working
And we can't stop now

Help us build this Bridge
Or stop our task
And be knocked off into the abyss.

FIRST FURROWING

The headlines screamed at everyone
And were snatched up.
Buses gulped and puked them.
Like bullets out of gangster's gat the people
Bore home hated home loved home stabbed home.
Buildings gathered their shoulders to sleep.
Like a spider
I fed upon the Daily Worker and our evening
You unearthed my eyes when I found you
The sidewalks were clouds
And the air rosepetals
And at my mother's table
Two generations ate her labor of macaroni and wine.
After I plowed new loam on the couch to Beethoven's
    Grosse Fugue
Under blood on the sky.
At the window in her room my mother stared into
    the future.
Twilight long ago stretched the Square into a morgue
And the morning hour divided us for a day.

GRIEF SITS ON THE WINDOWSILL

The afternoon is a cow's eyes
Vacant as eternity.
The wind plays arpeggios with the leaves.
Life has left a to-let card
But the curtain says it is not so.
Munich sells the peoples of nations to the Nazi maw.
The streets wear green silence
Where dogs claw the brain.
In each house sorrows are needles in the hearts
      of the tenants
And this quiet a loose chandelier about to fall.

FOR OUR DAILY BREAD

The wind is lonely
The moon a fisheye weeps
For the fleeing branches,
And when I open the door
From odor of dirty underclothes' hallways
Into the bud of evening
You were not you but me,
And I coiled in myself like a snake.
Bach is arguing
For the millions whose lives
Are chopped off in the middle.
Remember the face of the gasworker
Thrown at the bus driver,
A mound of dead growth
With two pieces of low burning coals
Lost as a clown's bewilder.
The dish is a flat tire
And my words are barbs hooked in your flesh.
The wind is lonely
And crying in the branches
And the earth a hole for abrupt deaths;
I stab all ugliness
With a kiss on your cheek
And when you caught my lips
Your face became a red moon
Sure of the tide.
But the wind is an orphan
And nightmares bloom in the world.

THE REIGN OF BEASTS

A pigeon's song drops on the threshold
And bleeds for three floors

The flesh of this house
Is a drum with quivering strings inside

Your resignation chips like seashells on the rocks
And the tide pounds your heart

The parasitic rich and their stool lackeys
Suck our bloodstream

The room is violet
And bereft of air
Your face broken dishes

In the coalmine of my look
This tenement is caught in the gullet of earthquake.

LOCKED IN BED WITH BRONCHITIS AND THE DOCTOR HAS LEFT WITH THE KEY

The room slept on a star
With the blinds drawn
Then the sun rose in a wine candle bottle
And held a fan of trees
Under its eyes with a rascal's grin,
The two windows vied with the mirror to steal
    Dirk's paintings
But the windows and mirror were cheated
Because the clouds picked up the sun and hid it
And blackbirds flew out of its fingers.
A house in one window
Lit its pipe before going to work.
Slime of jealousy squirmed at the bottom of one bottle
Then the thermometer tripped over the breath
And the morning ran down the street throwing stones
    at the fences.
The nurse with a nine months' baby in her belly
    kicking to get out
Attacked the claws and nails stuck in glue of the
    bronchia
And hunted the butterflies of the dust like a witch.
Frozen clothes on the lines are dead children swinging
    in a playground.
If you were a real nurse I would invite you to bed
    with me.
At noon the clouds splashed the sun at the room
And left for the Orient,
The bottle is now full with the wine of sunlight.
From my chest a tree grew.
The wind mined the diamonds of the snow and blew
    them to people's doorsteps.

The petals of a rose tightened around the room
Ashes fell from the sky
And covered the air with twilight
Bringing ghosts of first inhabitants to house windows
And tenements' magnets pulled their occupants home.
Two candle flames are a buzz of bees chewing the germs.
One bottle is a cave of stalactites,
The mirror a street in Port au Prince
And the other bottle holds a rite of voodoo Africans
    upon a drum.
The fang of the hidden west
Bit the earth
And the skin of the universe turned purple and black,
The ritual brought stars
And the footprints of caterpillar streetlamps.
Safe in a blackout room as childhood
I fished up the dream where it snapped off
While the wolves of the wind tore the windowsills with
    their teeth.

QUARREL

My head is a ball of lead,
I move in blind melancholy
With tongue glued to silence
Mutely alive and dead

The day broke in two
And the parts are the wound,
My moths died in your red
Joy and killed the joy
And your thought became a peasant's shawl
Over singing shoulders

Molasses chokes the floor
No word is said
Your wings are broken
And you become me
Suffering like a bird trying to fly
Not knowing why.
Your youth stuck in mud.

My legs feel like Socrates'
After he drank the hemlock.

Light is in the way
You are a thorn in my vein,
The paintings upsidedown,
Nerves tied to a knot,
And I am in the way of myself.

Molasses reach my knees
Time is a splinter in my eye
The bed a stone in my windpipe.
I am the snow
With sparrow's footmarks
Wanting to be the sparrow.

NERVES HANGING OVER TELEPHONE WIRES

The automobiles drive upside down
Pedestrians walk on their heads
Trees reach for the sky like the stubs of dead men
One clock says 4:15
Another shouts 11 a.m.
Cross eyed faces scattered like weather stricken leaves
Train schedules run backwards
People go to the wrong houses
Somebody's heart pulses in the gutter
Ignored by the rain and the passersby
The market place is an insane asylum
Of hands grabbing meats money stamps abuses
Women running through each other
Get there just in time to lose it
I am the string to your kite
Picking up food for the week
Hungry mouths are tied to feet like tin cans
Grass grows towards the earth's center
It is neither day nor night
Only a cross eyed clock
Cerebrums falling from the twilight
And pieces of people dropping on the sidewalks

LIVE CEMETERIES

I

Autumn leaves flee like mice
Before the ice of winter,
Time sits like a nightmare
On the corner
This late afternoon
Staring with the forgotten look of the past.

Scribbles hieroglyph the desolate hallways
Old rags and junk clutter the gaps of the skull
The smell sticks beneath the nails
The dank walls blind as despair are garbage pails
These and bent women's stockings hanging at death
Groove the cranium.

I am neither here nor there
You aren't,
The skeleton arms of the birch
Are rigid as a vein in quartz
And the twilight burns a hole in my mind;
My skin shrinks with memory of childhood
Under the sidewalks taut as the tightrope of the present
And my shadows are sweatshops tied to my ankles.

II

The need for bread seized ore from the marrow
And no grass wounds the eyes
But experience,
Corners of fears like aging flesh,
Landscapes of youth,
And parents' blood on kitchen floors.
Joints become warped as trees,
Arrows stuck in throats stayed there.
Understanding like miracles of new light
Lit the forehead.
That was yesterday
Not so long ago as a beetle's life.
Time hides a backyard of scars,
Exposes fever heat of war
Lowering more caskets out of these days
Into the graveyard
Bound to this history
In the volcano's belly
Consuming the corpuscles
Leaving the changed streets
A different look on the tenements
And new faces out of the old.

Night leaks out of these rat holes
And feet return at night.

WINE OF THE HEART

Window woman kiss woman rainbow woman
Whatever hour of the universe
Waiting for me

I looked for you in alleys
In the moon's room on a wave
In street secrets
I looked for you in dancehalls
At tables of cafes
In the snowflakes
In strange streets of strange cities
I looked for you in the spring sap in trees
In my mother's dream
In a thousand books
In dates
Under eyelids of closets
In Van Gogh's potato eaters
In the cello of Beethoven's archduke trio
In the jewel box of clouds
And found you in the people

My dance of happiness
Halos your head

Your sleep filled face of roses
With your valley of shadows
These moments of this age

In the chair of smiles
With a dream in your flesh

Window woman kiss woman rainbow woman

Hands of healing
My beginning and end

Mirror of my moods
With bottomless well
Of understanding

We shall be together so long
It will seem like yesterday
For the blood of the tenement stopped
And ours were the hands removing the knife.

PHOTOGRAPH OF STARVED CHILD DUMPED IN A BURIAL CART

No one recognizes you
Who can know you now

Child without name
Flesh once elastic and human
Born without being born
Stitch in the quilt of the dead and dying covering
 the earth

Bones sharp as the points of stars
Shriek of the bombed blood
Look for your mother
In the stones that do not see this picture news

Sleep
Target of the goose step and the ostriches
Child of man
Cinder bedded in the eyeball of the world

IN THE WAKE OF THE VULTURES

Big black shoulders carry the stars;
Alleys and streets vein the cities,
The lights blink afraid to open
Their fearful eyes.
Fat buildings shiver
And the inhabitants crouch in corners
Mostly silent and black
As the long narrow alleys.
Prayers in closets of loneliness
Plead against the pitchforking death.
Corners are nude
As penniless girls
And talk falls on the sidewalks
Like a black cloth.
Refugees wander through cities
With eyes like empty rooms.
Silence regiments skeletal ruins
And the underground plans
The sabotage in the bowels.
Fear is thick as a hidden club
And the goose-step tractors the looks
Of the citizens.
Queues like prisoners wait for the rations;
A brick smashes a Jewish window
Splintering the pupil of the city.
Like lightning the frightening wail of the sirens
Announces the vultures
Whose breath of death
Eat stones and rooms and the hunted
Leaving cavities in buildings
Like jumbled rows of decayed teeth.

The broken walls and the bones weep
While under the raped streets and the
Household furnishings in mid-air
The underground moves like unseen blood
Sharpening the weapons of revenge.

THE BALLAD OF THE BLACK IDEA

The brown cheeks of the woman
With the patched legs like sorrow
Holds in her mind
The gifts of clouds
Like a stored anticipation

Her husband with expensive TB
And fingers like penises
Brings to the second hand furniture
Pay envelopes containing rags

The shadows stemming from their house
Are hunger
And the rooms
Anchored to the cemetery

The Cross lies on her breast
Rooted in childhood and the Holy Book
Every Sunday Mass
Is a communion with God
Unseen as the current in the live wire

The clothes on the lines
Like the household's entrails
Drip anguish and troubles,
Morning words between piazzas
Excavate differences

The air is full of briars
Between them
The woman fights her neighbor
Whose eyes are a November
Of lonely gulls and iron

The woman's feet are without shoes
As the poor must always be with us
So must the rich
God has made the world a trial
To prepare us for the life after death

The neighbor spits at the woman
And threatens to cut God's heart out
And feed it to the pigs
For serializing wars
And keeping the people divided into classes

The woman with the sorry hair
And intuitive nose and brittle backbone
Says
God has a reason for wars
Man is inherently bad

The neighbor spits again
And her eyes answer
That the brotherhood of the countries
And the common ownership of the earth
By all the peoples
Will bury wars forever

The woman bristles with an unknown torment
In her dreams
She sees people happy
With houses food schools jobs and health
Having heaven on earth
She sweats with fear,
Coming on earth she loses this in Heaven,
She sweats in dreams
She sweats awake
Trapped in agony

The woman with patched legs of sorrow
And the gift of the next life
Despises her neighbor whose November eyes
Are lonely gulls and iron

TWILIGHT AND SUNRISE

The cold bitten feet
Hoof back and forth
Or travel in circles
Covering 25 miles
A day
50 miles a day
Conversing with other dogs
Shoulder to shoulder
Singing songs
That bind name to name
Close together
As atoms in iron
And our atoms
Are the descendants
Of the pickets
Back to the beginning
Of strikepangs:
The feet are proud
And after relief
Weary
The other 5 o'clock
Home going crowds
Make you feel homeless
Almost an outcast
With your family
Hanging in midair
Or stranded at sea
The dogs next morning
Travelling the circles
Protect the 5 o'clock crowds
The foundation of cities
The pay envelopes
Collective bargaining
The 40-hour week
The pickets with cold bitten dogs
Protect the air we breathe.

TO THE LEGISLATORS

    for passage of unemployment insurance for strikers

Like mad hornets
We will be thick in your hair
We will be ashes in your eyes
Our need like pneumatic drills unstopping in your ears
We will picket your houses
And light fires in your forgetfulness
And publish to the people
Your intrigues, your records, your lies,
Till you act for the people
Or we
Kick you out
With the toe of our votes!

FISHCUTTERS

the scales of the dawn
stick to the skin

of the cutters
ankle deep in fisheyes

white bony skeletons
sleep with them

and follow them
back to these wharfs

wet with the smell
of old love that anchors

them to the innumerable fish
that come forth

perpetually
and is their breathing

FOLKSONG

    I pass
by day
    and night
no one has
    seen me

    If you ever
want to find
    me
and know me
    leave behind
yourself
    and enter
the caves
    of other
people

    there you
will find
    me
who is
    yourself

DISCOVERY

for my son who saw a photograph of one of the victims of the last war, an Italian lad blinded and handless, learning to read braille with his tongue

do not cry
in your sleep
because the boy
has no hands

they are the wind
sprinkling seeds
in the crippled lands

do not cry
under the steps
because the boy
has no eyes

the refugee
has them

do not cry
when you wake
with the lamps
         dying
seeing the boy
reading braille
with his tongue

he is following
the feet of sandpipers

be not bewildered
by midnight
O child
weeping among
the weeds

look
hear
the dance of his flute

his stump is around
your shoulders

THE HISTORY OF A SHEET ON A CLOTHESLINE

the fences
partition the sky
putting miles
between tenements

the wind is homeless
and naked
perpetually rubbing its back
against the sheet
for warmth

that ground it came from
is almost in another
country
        now

in squat closed mills
where the air and sunlight
are barred out
fingers spinning and weaving
bring forth beauty
and die by machines
breeding families on the
nails of poverty

generation
       after
              generation

the night is raw
as the taste of pain
and the moon sees the sheet
and the cord it haggles from
restless on the nameless
night
agued with
the sweat of anxiety

the mad clutching of centers
the large bones of the
arthritic
the burdens of the tossing
sleepers
the cracking flesh and the
protests
of the newborn

dangling at the moon's edge
the ground hears
the quarrels in bed
the adolescent masturbating
the cheated turning to ice
for the love
that never arrives

flapping in the night
unable to shake off
the blood of the alarmclock
the anguish of the pay envelope
the unfulfillment of the years
and the dripping
blood
in the backyards

there against the nighthours
quivering
        sorrowing
dangling cold
flag
of the countryless
              inhabitants

TRANSMIGRATION

between the grey sea
and the overburdened sky

a seagull
and a man

dived into the water
that was chopping

the air
and swam

4 fathoms under
and when they came

back to the rock
dripping with autumn water

the seagull
was the man

and the man
the gull

A LITTLE AUTOBIOGRAPHY

a dog ran
down the night
with my left hand

I asked
the lamppost
where the dog had gone

the lamppost
hung its head
it had no tongue

I hunted
the dogtrack
down the endless night

and on a hill
I saw the dog
burying the bone
of my left hand
in the moon

WHERE I ONCE WAS...

where I once was
the shadow
lay behind me

now I am
completely
immersed
in the shadow

my left eye
is absent

and one half
of my body
from the head
to my feet
is no longer
with me

LAMENT

*(for the Gudrun, having pulled out
was never seen nor heard of again)*

the crew is water
sky or fishes
o nobody knows
the dragging dark
and the driftwood wabbles
of what ship
in the horizon's pupil
like a cinder
in the eyes of mourning
unable to cry
this day is another stone
falling in the well
hollow hearts
belly out like wishes
raking the watery
waste
and the stones pile
pulling down
the buoys of hope
was it Orion
lifted the seabird
or the moon
or fish people
on the seas' floor
after a sacrifice
or the Flying Dutchman
a mate
or death a living
token
to remind the dead
of the first life

nobody knows
but the crying gulls
the tongue–tied
wind
and the waves that wash
under
the past and the present
slapping against
the walls of the future
o to tear the trap
of the sea
and give them
another birth
o nobody knows
and the waiting

THE TINY ROOM

the tiny room
in the tree
is where
I live

I leave
with the dawn
key
and enter
with the moon

I have my supper
of minutes
and laughter
and exchange
tales
with my children

the factory
is in a forgotten
city

we dance
to the warbler's chant
and explore
the sky
take time
apart
and with singing
eyes
approach
the magic world
of sleep

wife and
mother
the air and the
open window

in our room
snug
in the tree
brew
        memory
with the moon

5

      I say this
so it sticks
in the mind's craw

each
      in his own
            weight
& specific
value

on his individual terms

to be hammered
out on the
      anvil
         of
experience

into his usable metal

thus
created
from his
ore

so each one
      counts

. . .

love does not
judge
      he

is
too busy
making

      anew

Grandmother and child
  sharing a private language
    have kings between them.

Some things I'm almost
  afraid to give thought or say —
    air is traveling.

As the keel of a
   boat is submerged in water
      so are we in death.

O let go, forget,
   pull up anchor and take off —
      the harbor rusteth.

Hark, who has looked on
   spring ice and not wanted to
      give away himself.

The pines, loaded with
   green and dew, and o our road
      going deeper in.

Moon in the river
   are as close as they'll ever
     join separation.

The sky's in us and
   snowing heavily — today
     is no longer here.

The extremities
   cross at the heart and listen
      to go on again.

The vision of God
   tying nature together —
      the air is on fire!

Cat in no one's yard
   licks peace and eternity:
     next life I'll have time.

I asked the apple
and the brook
behind the house
when
and they said
soon

as the bark contains
the tree
by holding the sky
good shelters
evil

Memory arrives
establishing the permanent —
what isnt
is most

Night is always thus,
prehistoric
chunk of iron
seen —
then, the
waiting

Too well
the buoy and anxious
light remember —
Night is double
deep

Sky is a jewel
and O
the snow firmament
I troll
thru bone-bare

the Road hurrying
to the outermost
inside —
odor of deep
sea

Live with division
o holy fragments —
pray for
Continuity

whatever is said
or thought
like a stone
thrown in a well
strikes
bottom

listen,
the whistling
from the flaming wood,
it's a cavebird
being fed

there is no ill
o Divine Integrator
you cannot heal
with joy

How cleanly it writes
on sky
this eel–grass
to conceal
the underneath

SUDDENLY SPACE . . .

Suddenly space is over all
isolating

the sky
those eyes

air
that stride

that skin
the blooming green

and all outside wanting
to be contained in a figure

A MAD ONE . . .

A mad one is planting
seeds of a pine forest
to astound the moon

god-obsessed
stalking without a tongue
the rooms of a special sleeping

even the night is with ague
knowing
and being a lamp

JOY!

Joy!
Maker and crown of all estates

as any forest
knows

THE PASSING . . .

The passing evenings
antique the seacity

memories are medallions
with zodiacs another age will read

the air is a person
held up by a forgotten prescience

with eyes
closeting strata of family

only the music of beholding moments
has value

giving interior of houses
a patina of poems

against a museum civilization
with its funereal body

IT IS THE LIGHTNING . . .

It is the lightning we live on
with no home
between white thunderheads

even as looking is
or with the sudden voice of the height
the ground is mobile

the river racing past
and caught on the blue wind
is the wind and that river

from anointed shadows
cathedrals rise
with held-in liturgies

an existence of that quality
before and after
thunderstorms

AT WAKE...

At wake of light
came a birdmusic
never before heard
delicious as coupling

and drinking the similitude
marvelling
with it
fell asleep

THE OTHER SIDE

>   for Betty Olson

Bury the women on their backs for the God of the skies
the men face down, the neither, standing —
and those who rise from death have the surprise
of three worlds within them, commanding

the earth is the center of the cosmos
with two visions, fact and the hidden
disclosing the unmanifest by losses
predetermined and left with gains forbidden

not knowing how we want it, anyway
it comes, the pith of it, hurt and be hurt
embody dis-similar natures, assay
that sparrow fluttering in and out of the dirt

beloved earth and ethereal look
laid out for the praisings of this quickening brook

THE GARDEN OF THE APOCALYPSE

The black man has no premium
on color and enslavement
neither has the yellow man, nor the white
nor the brown skinned

each person
carries a civil war within him

who wedding the contraries
in himself
already is on his way
pioneering the new civilization

flags are obsolete
and so are countries and creeds

we are witnesses and participants
ending an interregnum

tomorrow, no, today
Earth is the begetter of the universe
and Love, the only kingdom
which is not by fiat

a man is in it
outside it
or approaching the gates

THE GOLD

The suddenness flowers have
startle the air
with their fire and ether
as we do with what is ours
because we are
the gardeners of each other

OUD SONG

Strolling in the Rainbow Mist
in this hour of you
& Fitz-hugh Lane
and triste

ah to interslide as easily
as the waves do
moment by moment
their unceasing activity

Separated by a view
You with your shading & secrecies
always here and not here
& I wet as Moon dew

ASTEROIDS

It's one
Map of the Self

We are watching
one another's wake

A soul off center
has that nature

AN AUSPICE

You sought me out
a Red Sea
refugee
and we dined on 6 oysters for me
and alien corn for you
I took you to Singing Beach
the Moon was absent
It was a sucking surf
my arm around your infidel shoulders
yours ringing my back
I ready for your Wilderness
You for my wisdom
I took off your blouse your hip holsters
my shirt and pants
and my two necklaces
It was a hurricane
we held between us
I remembered the beads
the nightsands had gulped them
and in the morning rain
I knew I would find them
they were half buried in approaching tide
in that heavy downpour
Driving to save the ring of Isis
and the bull's prick
I heard a clacking noise
My windshield wipers stopped working
I was in your Red Sea

BALLAD OF THE POSSESSED

for two days I had not heard from
her nor him
and when he did appear
his cheeks were freshly scarred

when she came in
swaying high and low in her Persian skirt
I knew that she had had
the best of him

'but you should see the marks she has'
said he
and I blushed thinking of the skirmishes
they had in narrow places, O

these two are mad
and I love them dearly because they
have the beast in them
hunting in the tundra of hunger

a nimbus of the white fox has he
and she, the wolverine's desire
yet nothing human or animal
satisfy their appetite

an unholy pair
foraging where the other begins
or leaves off
for what neither has flares inside them

'lead us into Temptation' is his Commandment
hers, dictated by a natal Moon
and panting after each other's midnight
sleep on the skeletons of charts

some are seduced by these tempters
and a few fulfil self-prophecies
as they prowl the differences
warring and secure in their Lunacy

AFTER READING YEATS

I am at Loblolly Cove washing his rhythms out of my Ear
the salt drying my hair and lips

The wind has given me its clothes
fitting me back into my bones

My fire drives me
the world has my flesh on

THE TIDES

This plant we live with
has become a portion of our continual nourishing
and the direction it has taken is
the movement of flowing meetings polishing
the hours as the tides do —
and equal to the ocean's proffer —
a plant of functions
the leaves events, the branches thinking,
the loam in the clay pot
the flesh around this dreaming air
the plant loves in! The fur of the leaves
the skin of that invisible person
we are in the midst of
real as the upright plant the room is more for

SPADES

He rose like a golden phoenix
His destiny was hot upon his back
O He was chosen and He knew it

what beckoned Him, He was whirling
from the vortex of His own solar dominion
and a girl, for the girls

He had a wild grace and He had speed beyond the human
and the wicked Zebra he was master of,
what a glowing they drew toward them

those who could see went after
the god He had for anyone who
swept in His rays was made the same and special

He could straddle the Moon
and ride anywhere in Heaven
ah, how the other planets envied Him

He circuited the under-voyeurworld
and His spurs had diamond static
He had a secret the core of girls yearned for

He had tapped the firebox of the Almighty
and stolen His thunder and lightning
nobody knew except the girls and some freaks

His stride was more exciting than walking Space
and nothing was possible to stop Him
but the splash of an atomic brick

Evangel of His Epoch, He ended beside a dead girl,
His best friend blew taps on His old harmonica —
the mini-skirts, O they cried their hearts out,
      who had Him most

A WEAK LAMP

Madame Rosehips spies Sir Galahad
rowing up the Annisquam in his Half Shell,
she waves for him
and the swathe of that shadow
frightens him furiously onward

He's up against three swords
"Three? What three?"
His wife's beauty, her brains, and her wealth
"Ah" and in her mind
she is swiftly comparing her situation
"I did not know Galahad was married"
A common reincarnation
Remember how the baker smacks the dough?
"mmmm"
Well, a woman could massage
a man's acorns
skirt her breath upon them
"mmmm"
and then tuck them in her oven!
Her belly laughter rumbling
over the parapet and into the blue river below
"It can be done?"
Not you, Rosehips, you come on too strong

His last hope is to leave a signature
behind him

And a mean ancestor
"If he can swallow those three swords
stuck in his windpipe
they might melt
and he'll get his lost ball back"

How many
rip thru the second amniotic sack?

He thinks his cap of crazy bees is invisible

A jukebox historian
surviving on tv dinners
and borrowed light

ROCK VILLAGE

The Ancestral Genius edged over
                    (as the Sun came upon
the rowboat after, the lad's ashes fell upon her bosom again
and his father's ear drank them),
he waved his fist way out
over the Harbor
            the drool of his spittle
like a spider's wetness
clamped the village down hard
right thru the cellar
and onto the first Immigrants' Rock
((& underneath the moss
were the Mourners on the Sea's Hill watching the Nightsky
for a Barque's prow
                which went under us and swept us
into its belly)
        taking us with them))
the wind over the nightleaves
whipped up his Acid again
& splashed it against the windows of the newcomers

the bones of the buried barking
up and down
the chartreuse morning
and bedding down in the 500 year Nest
dear Bird
        whose shit is that on your tail
& way up there the heretic fulfiller,
                        'Narcissus has no equal'
& leaping out of the ashes
smearing his Ink on the Sky
                shaping

there the Images of his Ire
lessons for the fixed Illuminati

the three rivers a bloody Styx

in the Harbor
               an Asylum Barge is letting off
a breed of tin settlers

THE *THEIA MANIA* OF CHARLES OLSON

The torch went out
and it is Dawning in his NIGHT

                        the pillar that made the Matrix
gave breath up becoming the very Road itself

taking back
            the fountainhead of
                        ecstacy

and above
            pathfinders to origins to

the more we are ourselves
                        the more we give
breaking
            the darkness through
                        to this juncture:

The Feast of the Resurrection!

(who will ever forget
                    that crack in the sky
that heralding sunset of
                January 10th)

the eddies that his fist held slid
                        away
and some are pools of aqua vitae
in the woods of skulls

O Earth, receive him
he, who loved Thee
                with such outgoing
                and such a penetration

    fierce as devotion to
                    principle
    (as so few treaders of
                    this planet)
                                for
    reaching out to get that
                    inmost prize you hide

    Receive, dear Earth
                against
                        the despoilers
  this
        Quickener
                of Thee
  and Thine

              this central HUMAN figure!
              and His rhythms of creation

  To be

  alive as he!
              by tasting the ichor of his
                              Presence

PAEAN OF JOY FOR THE BIRTH OF A CHURCH

for Richard Emmanuel, a
Leonardo of Opposites

Because you staked a Cross-Roads
for catalyzing Chaos
the Devils genealogies erected came forth for a
    settlement

Because your X is such a battlefield for revelations
rip rapping torn egos, toppling Idols, fumbling
    among directionless statues

Because pariahs have an arena to be in

Because you are intoxicated with inmost gargoyles
and a wideawake-at-the-miracles-of-phenomena Child
as we are

Because the primeval is your quest
drawing faces out, penetrating the crookedness where love is
ever-ready for surprisings and the risks

We witness, participating in the death pangs
between that hidden instigator and the Big Vacuum
see-sawing with them and resting on the sidelines

We were with you when your father gave up his body
and entered your citadel
that each of you who had rejected the other
became for the other a keystone

And we were Annie, Diana, your mother, and the
    enclamped relatives
for when you buried him in the Bosom of the
    anointing Scheme
we, the left behind, were torches in your Womb
which you had relinquished for 2 days and night to watch
your father descend to another beginning

and no sound fell from your lips
and you, well on your own road
lonely amid the protocol usurpers,
the non-anvil Hierarchy

        wrapped in the luminous hood of non-interfering
we who were left felt that Transfiguration
as we enacted pieces of ourself
doing quietly what our instincts told us to,
Chanter Marston, Captain MaGee of the hurricanes,
Rob lute Hawkins, Dayle of the In-Kept Song, and I,
servicing the famished mendicants, star treaders,
        mid passage to autonomies
we were the tongues of
creating a world between words and silence

Because you were in the Arctic of two regions
and we were separated for the wilderness
a sea of Unknowing swayed the cradle we are
each lifted the Church off the ground
a clairvoyant Death
and the loving Spoke of it

THE NIGHT THE HARBOR FILL SAT ON THE COMMUNITY FISH PIER TABLE

It was a night of pre-Columbian mirrors
when reflections were epitaphs of position
It was a night of beggars and alms crawlers
It was a night of the long binoculars and needlepoint
It was the night of the shadow developers went crying
    door to door
It was State Rep. David J. Lane's and State Rep.
    Richard R. Silva's night
because they were caught pledging their vote to
    fictitious jobs
It was Alfred G. King Jr.'s night of the surreptitious ace
beside divine Judge Charles F. Mahoney
It was Martin Ray's night of ghostly fishes
It was Bradley Bell's and Mac Bell's night of the lead
    and the bronze
It was Salvatore J. Favazza's impossible possible date
It was Nancy Gray's turning the law to the key
It was a night unlike any Anthony Spatafora ever
    sparred with
and he has been to millennia
It was the night John F. Sheedy was caught with a
    plastic guppy in his coat
It was the night Albert H. Enos was told we are all in
    God's freighter and he didn't believe it
When Toby Pett's brain reheard the clatter of
    cliques and claques
It was the night Edward McLeod got stuck between
    boulders in a canoe of whitewash
It was the night before the night of Peter Watson's
    Olympian maneuvers
It was the night Larry Burns brought in the Labrador
    moratorium

It was a night Dianka Kwiecinski read her capsule
While Joe Wilkins blasted the ledge for the little boat
    owners
It was a night James Moses hung around the hot
    vestibules of the deep freezers
When Lawrence Purdy saw urban renewal black-balled
As Edward Welch hid behind his Mona Lisa moustache
It was a night Peter Tibbetts dropped anchor with
    Samuel de Champlain
When John G. Silva's binnacle was drunk shipping donkeys
And Joe Williams told us about a new species
It was the night John A. Foote was given a third shoe
It was the night of Rafe's Chasm and Donald Ross
It was the night Nick Parisi picked up his three boasts
    and went to the poorfarm for consultation
It was the night Stephen A. Moynahan Jr. sent an
    emissary Howard Richardson with 10 copies of
    an encyclical
It was the night Isabel Natti's heart pumped faith
    into legislation
It was the night George Polisson caught the train
    going forward backward
It was the night Ann Lloyd kept tossing for choices
It was the night Elizabeth G. Smith had a Karma shift
It was the night Robert Hawkins dreamt of his boyhood
    on the Dog Bar
It was the night of the painful lesson for Reps. Silva
    and Lane
It was the night Tim Sullivan had Bill Cahill on his back
It was the night Renee Gross delivered the impact the
    surveyors missed surveying
It was the night of billboard map when the minister
    without portfolio
showed the 'logical and illogical' in our dirty house

and how to cleanse the gunk off that sticks them together
for it was the night Emmanuel became Mother to the city
It was a night the state commissioners took joyfully
      back to Boston with them
It was a night all public meetings could be
      for that epiphenomenon still rocks my skull
and now that I have gotten the song of it out
I am freed

LENIN SPEAKS

Smash this frankenstein Mausoleum
let breath in my frozen corpse
for the Winds to free!

We were first to step off
the Globe
         and walk upon the OZONE!

and
    imagine
        me
        an IKON?

always these bureaucrats
capitalist,
      and now
            communist!

who have thick lenses that blunt the light
ears, stuffed with catechism

armed to the lips against any
and all
      unsanctioned
IDEAS

trespassers upon other lands

who think the REVOLUTION
is
  only
      ONCE?
ah,
    what surprises they are in for

IN THE WAKE OF NIGHT
I BEHELD THE GENERATIONS

                                        my sons, Suns!

                    I

Horses are full of winged wonder gathering
each other in
and staying as they are
                    as celestial earthlings
rejoicing as they do
and possessing
        them!

Each woman has within her
a stallion and a mare
and she will know which horse
you are unable to steer

you also have two horses within you
a mare and a stallion

the woman who sees that mare within you
will be driving her own stallion
spiking
all tender loam
for weeds in a field-time

your race of people have been ruled by the
                                Mare

the stallion is the head
the mare the heart
for her the stallion is her Will

to master that animal within you
is what
your life is all about

you
    determine this by your vigilance upon yourself
your survey and
            interpenetrations

if she is on her stallion
know it
dont become the mare to a mating of contraries
in the Crucible of the Unseen
for the taming of the two
            Within

because the meaning is mastery

II

Be wary of this mare within you
the Heart
let it not have the reins
or her stallion will mount you

face this god
      and controlling
           be doubled!

as originals
and the not you for her
the not she for you

women mistaking gentleness for weakness
have their black steed thriving on fire and smoke
trampling upon the mare within them
when you have lost your iron
upon it
and reacting ruins of relationships
accompany the days and years ahead
and behind has a life of its own

                    (the light of her
                                your flame)

watch the flood-tides of the heart
they sweep over seeing beaches and stout marshlands
and blinding waterglow prevails

women whose stallion is their innermost nature
saddle a man-mare estranging
both
and a plague invades the household —

ah the lesson of cuneiforms on the chromosomes
with their urgings
not for you/
itself

the spoken
        each hears differently

be a friend
to this mare within you
but let it not
lead you
                (the dark of you operating in the other)

though the heart and head
are engaged in a contest
and the hidden near
                a serpent eye
inlaid with cunning

your power is your heart-mind
hers, her mind-heart
her sex and your head
dovetail
her head and your sex

remember your hands and stirrups
the tenderness
            in them
bringing her for each of you

never forget
this unruly pair
who and where they are/
testing the
        Within
              and the outcome

with time we learn
some late
              some soon
some never and beaten back to dust —
and each generation
appearing for the trial
with these Four Horses of the Apocalypse

fortunate are they
who make with a mate
the invisible Body between them

THE TWO HARBORS OF GLOUCESTER

The homecoming rascals with twilights and pearls

Peacocks of the Ocean!

A playground of the mind,
                        Ben Smith
or a rats' theatre

By any promontory,
                fish view
                            or town landing
the evershifting Hebrew sky

Who has not bumped upon
                       St. Charles
quicksilvering?

Under the sands,
            moon-masts,
murmuring voices

Peter Anastas
      a compass for following through
the continuity of the child

And granite Lane,
     Sitting Judgment,
                     the ultimate
    loner

Out of a joint death,
               in a Barque
                         his own hands wrought

birds of Christ!
      Betsy and Larry Scotti

Black Iris
      among the brier

Words,
        the real estate

Master mariner of fogs,
              springsong

In a soul's nor'easter,
            fishing the body up,
                        and the City!

Against the names,
            the uncommunications,
                      the undone

the triumph of Soothsaying
              Waters

The tears of the Mother of Good Voyage
                        wild roses

on the eyes of the lost
            who see in the dark

Navigating the millennium,
        the Parsons,
                Pole Star natives

at the Wolf's cunabula

City of the Chosen!

Fanatics at any
            angle
                  bound and free

as the galaxies
            whorling

around
        a Serpent Fire

The arrival of GIVING
                a fulfilling people

FIRST FREAK VILLAGE

I exercise my
Soul
on the snows of Cranes
beach

&
my body
in the sky's
retina

and
then rest
on the thighs
of Argilla
Farm

at Starfall
I unhinge
the streets of Old Tales
awaiting
me

the Citizens
iceskating
on the handwriting of

the vanishing
Days
healthy as horse
manure

the unripe and the middleaged
dream of a Frigate
Hero
and daily cling
at ghost grass

the Square thrums
on dirty rumors

chimney flues
have pulsing persons

there's a detour
at Religion

skulls in coffins
cackle by
radio

the Ipswich River
has taken
me
Underground
to do its psychography

TONGUE II

It is as sweet as the fountains of the two faced
this enamourer has tales before
and after the death of things

an evil Destroyer who has no endings
and its Maid of the Sky loosens a Firebird from the
       white ashes
for roosting people for a Loving they cannot conceive

nothing in all the Mystery of this Hastening Away
can measure its imperium
when it is resting an eternal Blackness sucks us in for more

it is the intimate of no entrances
this enamourer has one name and all others who had been
or ever will be

it follows the Lessons of metal, the Communion of
       minerals and plants
the Gradations of mankind, the Subtleties of the Spirit
and it leads to a speaker and listener who is the unity of
       Nature

the decades of the Machine Time, the blight of the printed
       word
are a black soot blown under
and the inner night space of the spoken is heard again

ELEVEN

                                      phosphorescence

I pull the plug out at 5
and all the nightbirds start whistling in my ears
trade is arrested
my hands forget the table
I'm in the bell throated song

the stars sway and the tower quivers
among them
spying out the black spaces in the music
the night is ours
and so are the throbbing arrivals and lucky squalls

the Dogbar's red flame
a bird's eye hub to the wheeling lives
the harbor is a lost
scarf of the disembarking fishermen and an old door
now as the returning sea

this Diamond less than a ball field
a telescope mound and a microscope mind
the beach sand and heather listening
around it, these and the awakened beam furtively curious
as if looking is all

LIBRARY OF DAVIDSON COLLEGE